Table of Contents

Introduction

'Now' is the right time to get started.

What holds you back from starting your own business? What holds you back from following your dreams?

People are often concerned that it's too late to start a business and that it's hard to do. Let me tell you something - every year there are over 500 new millionaires in this world; are you ready to become one of them?

If the answer is 'yes', then you need to get moving right now.

You don't have to be an expert, and you don't have to be perfect in what you do; you only need to be committed to what you do. You have to always push and move on, no matter what happens. Nobody said that it will be easy to become an entrepreneur.

This book will unveil some of the secrets that an entrepreneur needs to succeed and it will also reveal my personal experience and thoughts regarding entrepreneurship.

Every success story has a beginning. So, are you ready to get started?

Chapter 1: 10 Solid Reasons to Start an Online Business

The internet is expanding, companies are expanding, the population is growing and everything gets harder as time goes by. Nowadays it's much, much easier to start an online business rather than a physical one, and I will explain why.

1. Unlimited space - on a website, blog, YouTube channel or any other online platform by any means gives you unlimited expandability; you are not limited by the size of your business.

2. Global reach - if you start an online business, you have the whole world at your fingertips. It's just a matter of time until people discover you and your services. To achieve that you need to work, to invest and to commit to it.

3. You don't need to pay rent - to run a physical business, you need to buy or to rent a space, which is very expensive and it gets even harder to obtain profits.

   An online business requires a website which you won't pay more than $500 per year for (for the biggest possible website). You can pay anywhere from $20 a year to $500 a year. Some websites cost more to have security, e-commerce platforms and other additional plugins, but regardless, it's a lot cheaper than a physical place.

4. You pay less in taxes - one of the major reasons why people aren't making profits is because they need to pay most of their earnings to the state. An online business also needs to pay taxes, but the fees are lower.

5. You are in control - you are responsible for everything that happens and you control your whole business easily.

6. You don't deal with clients directly - everything happens online - purchases, refunds, customer support, everything - you won't have to deal with all kinds of people in person.

   It's simple - you buy something, and if you like it, OK; if you don't you refund it and that's it. In the real world, dealing with physical clients most of the time will give you headaches.

7. Unlimited growth - you can scale up your business however much you want - it's up to you how many platforms you want, how many websites you build, how many people you hire, how much you are aiming to earn. You can scale

everything up easily, as you are not limited by a space or a rent, and you pay less in taxes for everything that you do.

8. Flexibility - an online business can be run from anywhere in the world; you can work from an island, you can work from home, you can work at a coffee shop, you can work while you are in an airplane, you can work from wherever you want, and whenever you want.

9. You have more free time - running an online business isn't easy, but you can take a day off whenever you want if you feel sick or you need to solve something urgent.

The same thing applies to vacations; if you feel like you need to take a week off, you can do that without telling your boring boss about your problems.

10.   Less stress - you won't have someone who will tell you what to do, and you won't have deadlines given by somebody else; only you. You still need to fix some deadlines for yourself, but if you don't manage to fulfill one, nobody will fire you.

These are the reasons that made me switch from a mediocre job to an expandable and enjoyable business, which I can run with an army of freelancers who I don't personally know.

There are other advantages as well, such as paying a freelancer for what they do, not hourly. Paying someone hourly will lead you to increased expenses, wasting time and more. It's simple - you give someone a task to complete and as soon as they finish (no matter when - in 10 minutes or 3 days), you pay them.

When you work for yourself, you get paid by the results and not by the total number of hours that you work, so you need to schedule some projects that you need to complete each month to earn more money and to grow your business.

I believe that this is the future for smart entrepreneurs - flexibility, growth, self-improvement, value, money, travel, and a challenge.

Chapter 2: The Entrepreneur's Money Blueprint

Each person sees money differently. Each person has their own way of spending money, of earning money, and each person has a different 'relationship' with money. Most of the people have the wrong beliefs regarding money, beliefs which can ruin their entire life, just because the mindset is wrong. Here is the real mindset for money making entrepreneurs and for any other person:

1. To become rich, you DON'T need to struggle and go through a lot of pain.

People think that it takes a lot of work to become rich, just because they have to struggle, or to face different problems. Well, it won't be too easy, but if you really want to, you can do it. You don't to need to work hard, you need to work SMART; find a profitable business which brings a lot of money in, expand it, and you will become rich. Some say, "No pain, no gain"; this means that you have to put some effort in until you get there, but again, you need to work smart all the time.

2. "I don't know if I'm good enough"

You need to feel as blessed as any billionaire or other wealthy person. Wealthy people don't have something more special than you, they just found a way to discipline themselves; they worked and committed to something. Every human being has the same potential; it's all about PERSEVERANCE.

3. "To get rich, you need to use other people to accomplish your goals."

Hiring other people to work for your projects doesn't mean that you are taking advantage of them; you are actually offering them a job, a place to work. You need to help people and to add value (check the chapter "Help other people"), and as Richard Branson said, treat your employees like your best friends - respect them, laugh with them and they will also respect you. You will help others grow, earn money, earn a living, offer them a place to learn new things, and you will NOT take advantage of them.

4. "~~I don't need a lot of money.~~"

Oh, really? You don't need money, but you are dreaming of going on a fancy vacation, you want a car, you want something that makes you happier and guess what - you can't afford it.

Let's put it in another way - you are used to living paycheck to paycheck, you get into debt, you can't afford any more things, you are at the borderline and...you get really sick, you break an arm, or something bad happens to your family. What are you going to do?

Whether you like it or not, you WILL

NEED money all the time to live. Having more money will allow you to live easier.

5. ~~Struggling for money can cause health problems and it can get stressful.~~

Health must not be neglected; make sure to exercise every day, to eat healthily and to take time for yourself. Work hard, work smart, but take some time for yourself. Having more money will allow you to solve any health issues easier - you can buy healthier food (which is more expensive), you can go relax (massage, swimming pool, therapy, yoga), you can take a break (travel); you can do many things for yourself if you have MONEY.

6. ~~I don't have a degree, I can't become rich.~~

Bill Gates and Steve Jobs dropped out of University or College and they were billionaires. In fact, Bill Gates became the wealthiest man on Earth for several years and he still is in the top 5 billionaires on the planet. Again, becoming rich is all about COMMITMENT. With the right mindset and strategy, you can start an online business today. Invest in it, hire other people and results will start coming. Every person on this planet has this chance; the only reasonable question is "Do you want to become rich?"

7. ~~I am not smart enough to become wealthy.~~

I think most of us have the required intelligence to start a business; it's all about discipline. You can start learning today, and you can start making a plan today; then you just need to follow it. I had several plans in my life before I finally decided on something and now I am committed to it. I feel blessed to have my own business today; even if I struggled for a few years, I also learned new things from my previous experiences. Everything that you do is an experience and you always have something new to learn from what you do. The condition is to keep learning, keep working, keep growing.

8. ~~It's not fair to be rich while others are poor.~~

Being poor or mediocre will not give you the possibility to help other people; in fact, you'll barely have enough money for yourself. In case something bad happens to you, somebody else (who is wealthier than you) will need to help you. If you have money, you can help other people: you can donate money to the poor, you can start a fund raising campaign, you can build a school, you can do a lot of things to help other people – all with the help of money. Bill Gates donated more than $20 billion to the poor.

9. ~~It's too late for me to start a business.~~

NOW is the time to start a new business. You have the biggest tool in human history - the internet – so you have access to the global population, not just the local one. You can find a small niche which can bring you money even when you sleep! You can build a physical business which also uses the internet to expand. I've seen a lot of people working in a building, such as my cousin - she is an accountant for a travel agency in London. She has a few co-workers - a designer, a promoter, an IT specialist and her - the accountant. They sell everything online: packages, vacations, plane tickets, etc., and the company is 2-3 years old. The owner is making a lot of money and he's traveling the world while managing his business from a laptop. Nice, isn't it?

It's never too late to start a business; you can come up with a new idea which can change the industry, you can make a small business which just delivers a few services, and you can do a lot of stuff online (LEGALLY).

10. ~~It requires money to make more money.~~

Wrong again. You can start a business with no money, like I did. I started a publishing business: I wrote my books, I designed my covers, and I did not invest in anything at first. After that I started to invest where I could, and I have started to grow faster.

You can find lots of other ways to start a business with no money. You are not late and you don't need money to start a new business. All you need is to start.

Chapter 3: Why I chose to become an entrepreneur

Things have changed quite a bit in the past few decades; the world has evolved, technology has embraced our lives and new opportunities have been born.

Let me tell you something about myself - my name is Ryan (Razvan – my real name in Romanian, translates into Ryan in English and it's much easier to read and remember), and I live in Romania, Europe. Believe it or not, this is a poor place with all kinds of people - from gypsies to scientists, from monkeys to highly educated gentlemen.

My parents are both automotive engineers; I am myself also an automotive engineer and I am 23 years old. I was raised in more than decent conditions. We own a house, a flat, 4 cars and we have a small company which my parents run.

Since I was child, I loved to make MONEY. When I was 16 years old I signed up for Federico Mahora to sell perfumes to friends and other people - it was quite OK at that time. As my friends were just playing World of Warcraft, FIFA or Counter Strike, I was finding more profitable ways to spend my time. I was making around $100 a week profit and I also received gifts from the company for myself (perfumes, body creams, etc.). It didn't take too much to realize that I don't want to be a perfume reseller in my 30s, so I thought that I should do something else.

When I was 18 years old I immediately created a bank account and I signed up with PayPal and eBay. I started to buy stuff from China to resell here in exchange for a commission. I did this for around 2 years while I was in the University - as a student, it was OK, and I was making some pocket money - I was able to buy gas for my car, a laptop, go on a vacation, buy clothes and hang out with friends. At 20 years old, I wasn't thinking of more, even if I could have done it.

My English level and my overall education level were very high; I am certified international with a C1 level in English by Cambridge Essol Examinations (UK English) which means that my English level is advanced, close to a native level. Even if my University was in Romania, all my courses were in English; I chose to do this to further improve my English skills. At some point, I had enough of selling things and I found out that shifting to making money online would be a great idea which had a huge potential.

I immediately created an account on Freelancer.com and I started to write articles for an Indian forum, as well as for a blog which needed articles about football and slots. I was working over 4 hours a day and I was paid $3/ 500 words of original content. The people that hired me for this were really pleased and overwhelmed by how good my articles were. They were wondering how I could provide them such flawless articles for such a small price. Well... I am living in Romania, a place where the average national salary is 400 EUR, so earning $200-300 from home, writing from wherever I want, whenever I want, was Heaven on Earth for me. I did this for about a year, when the people that hired me thought that they could pay me $1.5/ 500 words and I refused; it was simply too low.

Then, I decided to focus only on University - I was studying Engineering, and I had projects which were really time consuming and that I had to put a lot of effort into to finish them on time.

As other friends were graduating, they weren't able to find a job or even if they did, it was poorly paid and very stressful. Even my parents used to work 8 to 10 hours a day at their jobs and earned around $800-$900. It wasn't bad compared to other salaries here, but compared to others from Europe or the United States, it was less than a laundry man would earn. Of course, expenses are bigger in countries where wages are bigger.

I thought... Hmm... I really need to find out a way to make money; a way that is legal, a way that could give me free time, a flexible schedule and also could give me the possibility to expand however I want. After a year of struggling, I found a solution (by mistake). How did I find it?

My best friend is a web designer; he now has a company which he runs and he decided one day to create a course on Udemy. He also told me that if I want to create a course about anything, just to have a look at the website. And I did.

On the homepage of the website, there were announcements and promoted courses. One was about Kindle Publishing and a small light bulb appeared above my head. I read forums, tutorials, websites, even books on Kindle to find out everything about this business and I decided to take a shot.

This happened almost 1 year ago. My first books weren't very well-written, and I was just running after money, but I soon realized that if I wanted to make money, if I wanted to deliver value to my customers and become an Authority, I had to adopt a new method - quality. A good quality product plus advertising are the only 2 things that you need to start building an audience.

Of course, writing books isn't the only thing that caught my attention - right now I am in the process of creating a blog; I want to create a course, a podcast and maybe a YouTube channel to get in touch with people who like what I do, what I write about and what I think.

If Justin Bieber can have his own fans and haters, well, I also want some fans and haters; why not?

Now let's get into the meat - what's the whole point of my personal life story? The point is - I am not like everybody, I've always been different than others, I've always been looking for ways to make money and ways to improve myself, and I like being an example to others.

I suppose this is due to the education that I received from my parents. I like to work hard, but for myself, not for a boring and stressful boss. I like doing new and challenging things, not doing the same thing from 9 to 5 for 30 years.

I want to afford everything in life, not to be cut off from what I love doing. I want to live life to its highest levels and I believe that one of the ways of doing this is exploiting the internet and doing great work which will last for years. I want to create an online Empire, a passive business to which I need to dedicate each day, even if I don't have a boss.

Even if you now think that I am very young to give advice to people, I think that my visions of life can give you some ideas about what you should do to get started with online entrepreneurship.

In the next chapters, I will discuss what it takes to be an entrepreneur, what the advantages are, how to adopt the right mindset and what kind of activities you can pursue.

Chapter 4: What does it take to become an entrepreneur?

What does it take to become a successful entrepreneur?

This is a very thoughtful question which is frequently asked by most people. Being an entrepreneur sounds nice, but it isn't easy at all. It requires a lot more than you think to become an entrepreneur, especially a successful one. If you are going on this path, nobody will guarantee you anything, nobody will care about what you do or if you succeed, and nobody will give you any advice about what you want to do. You need to figure out for yourself what works best and what doesn't.

Entrepreneurship is very complex, but it needs to be simplified to obtain the best efficiency, the best possible productivity level.

Imagine yourself being successful

First of all, before you decide what to start with as an entrepreneur, you need to see yourself in the future - if you start doing what you want to do as an entrepreneur, how do you see yourself in the future? In 1 year, in 2 years, in 5 years? You need to see yourself as a successful business person right before you start, and you need to keep that in mind all the way through your journey towards success. It's not easy, not everyone can do it, but you need to know what you want to achieve. You need to be positive all the time and whenever something is holding you back, you need to focus and to keep moving forward.

It would be nearly impossible for you to be in a good position 2 years after you start your own business if you don't imagine yourself as a successful person. When I started this whole concept, which at first I was just dreaming of, I didn't actually think that it would be that difficult. But... Here's the bad news - it's a lot harder than I thought.

Make a timeline with what you want to achieve.

Most people skip this essential step and it's one of the biggest mistakes that you can make. What are you fighting for? What are your goals? You need to think wisely and to set goals for yourself - daily goals, monthly goals, yearly goals. You need to make a schedule for yourself and you need to respect it. If you don't, the only one you will be fooling is YOU.

When you work for a company and you're paid per hour, it doesn't necessarily matter what you achieved; it matters how many hours you work and you actually don't care too much about what happens next. When you work for yourself, you need to focus on finishing tasks and not how much time you work. Money will come as soon as you finish your tasks –

the more you finish, the more money you make.

Dream big, start small

You don't need to invest your whole savings into something or to hire dozens of people starting with day one. You need to start with small steps, but you need to have the big picture in your mind all the time - you need to set a destination which is far away, but you have to travel slowly and constantly.

Pay attention to details

What a lot of entrepreneurs do when they work on a project is to rush everything, even if they know that this is sometimes one of the worst things. Whenever you work on a project, make sure to pay attention to details, take your time and create something great for your customers. What's key here, is to keep an eye on your rivals and study their flaws, and then from those flaws, try to create something which excludes them. Nothing is perfect in this world, but at least try to maintain some high standards for everything you do.

Wake up early

Ugh... Waking up at 6:00 AM... Sounds painful, but I'll tell you what - it isn't. You just have to get used to it, even if it's difficult at first.

I'm not sure if you noticed, but some people manage to get a lot more out of one day. Have you ever wondered how they do it? Well, by using proper time management techniques, and believe it or not, waking up early is by far the best technique.

If you wake up at 11:00 AM, you'll be sleepy all day, you'll have headaches, you need to eat, to take a shower, to get dressed and guess what... It's already 1:00 PM. If you need to do any other stuff in your home - take the dog out, go shopping, do some cleaning...

Your day is already done. By the time you finish all these, your energy is wasted and you won't be able to achieve anything that you wanted to.

The human body was naturally "programmed" to get rest between 10 PM and 5 AM in the morning. This is the best time schedule. Imagine that you get up at 5:00 AM, you take a 2 minute cold shower to get your blood moving, you drink some water, you get dressed quickly and you go for a short jog outside while it's still cold and quiet. You need just 10-15 minutes of doing this every morning.

Don't take this as weight loss advice (even if it helps that too); take it as a health and energy boost for the whole day. When you finish this, it will be around 5:30 AM - now go eat something healthy, take a short break and at 6:00 AM you will be fully loaded for work.

Write, read, manage your activities, finish your payments, record a video, post an article on your blog, do whatever you have to do from 6 to 10 AM without any breaks. Have a break, relax your mind and then continue whatever you have to do.

After 12:00 PM you can do your other daily activities which I mentioned at the beginning - do some cleaning, shopping or other activities of your own.

In this way, you get the best out of a day and you also have a healthy life - you sleep 8 hours, you wake up early, you do some morning exercise, and you work in the quiet while everybody sleeps (no one will disturb you at 5:30 AM - no Facebook, no phone calls, no messages, no noise from the street; everything is quiet).

If waking up at 5:00 AM is too much for you, you can wake up at 6:00 AM or even 7:00 AM, but no more than that. Imagine that if you had a full time job, you'd have to wake up at 7:30 AM to get ready for work. In this case, you do the same thing, but the only difference is that you work for yourself, and not for anybody else.

If you take a look at most of the successful entrepreneurs, you will see that they have a very well-organized timetable; they wake up early and they work all day long, starting from 6:00 AM.

From my personal experience, before I made a schedule for myself, I was being constantly disturbed by other people (friends, family, other people, phone calls, Facebook announcements, invites and the list goes on).

As most of my friends wake up at 10:00 AM during weekends, until that hour I am capable of working at least 3-4 hours before they start calling to hang out for a coffee.

Constantly improve yourself

If you have big goals in life such as achieving the status of a millionaire, you need to change a lot of things before you get there. You need to understand that you need to discipline yourself and to commit to something. When you start earning money, start improving yourself - the more money you make, the more you need to focus on your self-improvement.

When you earn a couple of thousands of dollars, you need to read at least 1-2 books a month about personal growth, business, investing, new techniques, new ways to diversify your income, ways to preserve your income and efficient tips to manage money. No matter how much money you make, if you don't use it wisely, you will get into debt quickly.

When you reach milestones such as $10,000 or $20,000 or more, you need to get a private coach, attend private meetings, conferences, seminars, and webinars - invest in yourself.

Warren Buffet once said that nowadays, one of the best investments which you can make without risking to lose it is to invest in yourself.

I must admit that anything that you learn in life, whether you're an engineer, a doctor, or a lawyer, you always have to learn something new - this is what life is about. It's about constantly learning new things; the more you learn, the more you can do, especially in business.

Surround yourself with successful people.

It is said that a person has a combined character of the top 5 people who they are spending time with.

Try to fill those 5 spots with friends with a success story behind them; learn from their successes and failures and try to achieve success your way. Meet other successful people, attend seminars, listen to podcasts, and just try to follow people from which you can always learn something new.

Think twice

A real entrepreneur is careful with his money and he always thinks twice before spending money. If you are the type of person who earns $5,000 and spends $5,000 to "celebrate", well...it's not the best thing to be proud of. An entrepreneur will always be afraid of losing his money, an entrepreneur will always want to expand and grow his business, and an entrepreneur needs to take risks every time it's necessary.

You don't have to be perfect; a lot of people don't want to do something because they're afraid they're not perfect. "I can't do this, it's too hard for me", "I can't do this, I don't have the skills", "I can't do this, I can't find the time" - these things make you a dabbler, a person who gives up in advance.

The only thing that matters as an entrepreneur is to keep moving - you will make mistakes and you will learn from them, you will face problems and you will need to find a solution. Everybody faces these problems, but answer this question to yourself - if somebody can do it, why can't you? Why can't I?

Take risks

An entrepreneur takes risks (wisely), thinks twice before taking action, studies competition, comes up with new ideas, works on daily basis, constantly improves himself/herself, always asks questions, wakes up early, has a healthy lifestyle and much, much more.

Chapter 5: Just Start

If you have an idea which can make you a millionaire, if you have a vision in which you know that your success is almost guaranteed, just go ahead with it. Get started.

Most people don't take this step because they're afraid of what will happen. They're afraid that they won't succeed, they think that somebody else already got there, they're afraid that there is nothing certain for them, and they think that if they want to start something, they have to be perfect.

But you know what? Nobody is perfect.

You don't have to be perfect, you just need to push the 'Start' button in your head and get moving fast. Obstacles will come into your path; it's normal to be that way. You will make mistakes, everybody does; it's something natural from which you have to learn. Mistakes are meant to improve ourselves, to learn how to avoid making the same mistake again.

Choose something in your life that makes you happy. Choose something for which you were meant to live. If you have a passion for something, find out how you can turn that into a sustainable business; find out how you can combine success with joy and get to work!

Are you feeling down or not sure of what you are doing? Are you feeling that your idea isn't good enough?

Let me tell you something - whatever you do or whatever you are willing to do, make it PRO. Make it big, make it happen!

Don't worry, everybody has ups and downs, everybody has their bad days, but it doesn't mean that you have to give up.

Chapter 6: Motivate yourself – sources of motivation

Life is a challenge; a challenge which not everybody likes, a challenge for which not everyone is ready. But what if... You become the challenge for life?

Motivation is the major player in achieving success. You need to be a highly motivated person to keep moving on, no matter what results you get, no matter what problems you face, no matter how hard it gets - you need to keep moving on towards each checkpoint of success.

How can you actually do that? You need to find internal and external sources of motivation of your own which will last long-term (even for a lifetime).

Before you make a list of internal (emotional) and external sources of motivation, you need to analyze your passions and dreams. What are they? Write down everything and analyze them carefully.

Internal (emotional) sources of motivation:

- You want to prove to everybody that you are the best
- You want to get popular
- You want to help other people - build a school, donate money
- You want to impress women/men
- You want to invest in yourself (courses, seminars, self-help strategies, etc.)
- You want to feel like you are 99% better than other people
- You want to be confident
- You want to be financially free
- You want to meet successful people
- You want to meet specific people who are popular
- You want to get married
- You want to help your family
- You want to help someone
- You want to have a fit body

- You want to meet the woman/man of your dreams

External sources of motivation:

- You like cars and you want to buy a brand new supercar
- You like IT and you want a brand new, high-performance computer
- You want the latest tech in your home - smartphones, smart TVs, audio systems, gadgets and other accessories
- You want a fabulous house - a mansion
- You want to travel the world, to see each part of it
- You want to buy things which make you happy
- You want to become a millionaire

Other Sources

- Find an idol, a mentor, a person who will drive you up towards your dreams
- Work until your idols become rivals

You can't achieve all of these at the same time, so you need to set some goals - this month I want to buy a suit, next month I want to buy a new computer, this year I want to buy a new car, in the next 3 years I want to own a house, in the next 5 years I will become a millionaire, etc.

Even if these sound simple, finding sources of motivation is highly efficient for personal and business growth.

Note - When you will be making a lot of money with your business, you will buy anything that you want, but at some point, you will get bored. Then, what will you do? The best long-lasting sources of motivation are the ones in which you receive emotions - such as helping other people or your family, etc. If you use all your money just for personal purposes, at some point you will get bored of living the "wealthy" life.

If you take a closer look at a few popular millionaires, or even billionaires, such as

Bill Gates, he has donated billions of dollars to charities, to children from Africa, to students who want a private scholarship and much more. Making others happy and giving them unique life opportunities will give you the best feelings in the world.

After all, this is what life is about: having the ability to help others, while being wealthy and enjoying your own life.

As a personal example for sources of motivation - I am an automotive engineer and I graduated from a computer science high school - I like innovation, performance and futuristic gadgets - this includes smartphones, cars, and computers, and I also enjoy traveling. I would love to have the latest MacBook PRO with the ultimate specs, with the latest iPhone with the ultimate specs accompanied by the latest Android smartphone.

In the automotive industry, I would love a V8 engine to hear how it roars each day under the hood; I love the power, the feeling, everything. I would love to see the whole world (safe zones), and I would love to have all of these at the same time if possible, something like cruising in a V8 convertible car (Audi R8 Spyder, BMW M3 Cabrio or Mercedes Benz SL500 - I am a fan of German cars) in Europe for 1 month without stopping - every 3-4 days a new city to visit.

How does that sound?

I think it sounds like motivation, dreaming, and seeing the future ahead of me. For all these dreams to be accomplished, we need money; to get the money, we need to work smarter and harder.

Find what motivates you, what drives you crazy, set goals and get to work!

Chapter 7: Believe in yourself

Scientists have proved that 80% of a person's success is based on what that person thinks about the business or, in other words, how much you believe in your business and in yourself. If you are motivated and committed enough to keep moving, to keep working hard until you reach all your goals, then you are unstoppable.

The main reason why people are failing with their businesses is not because their idea isn't good, it's just because they weren't committed enough to what they were pursuing. If you adopt the right strategy, the right mindset and you put it into action, you can't lose. Even if you do a thing that everybody does such as YouTube videos, if you adopt the right strategy, if you invest a little bit in advertising and equipment, you can't fail. Every year new YouTubers are getting rich just because they have the right mindset. This requires some skills though, but you can learn everything, if you want to. Nobody was born 'experienced' or 'blessed' or 'lucky'; most of the luck is determined by your own actions.

Believing in yourself will give you the power to keep moving on, no matter how hard it gets. After all, that's all that matters - how much can you withstand to keep moving on? Winners face a lot of issues and difficulties until they become winners. Success doesn't come by blinking an eye once or twice; success is something which talks about yourself.

Believing in yourself will allow you to improve yourself, to adopt new strategies, to change plans, to work harder and to learn how to compete with others, because whatever you do, it won't be easy. Life is a jungle, and the internet is a jungle where other people will 'hunt' for results, for money, or for success. Are you going to be prey or a predator?

Each of us has ups and downs, but that doesn't mean that you have to give up; you need to find new, innovative ways to continue. Just take a look at the big companies - they always compete and keep up with each other (such as Samsung vs. Apple); neither of them settle, neither of them give up, they just keep moving on, each of them having different marketing strategies and both of them successful.

Competition is something which you need to dominate. It will always exist; whatever you will do, you won't be the only person who is doing that. There will always be someone else who is doing the same thing as you. The wheel isn't reinvented, it's just being painted in different colors by someone else.

From competition a new process is born - innovation. If competition didn't exist, we would have the same things for decades, for centuries even, but as competition is a major player in most businesses, to keep up being successful we need to come up with new, innovative ideas. But all these ideas wouldn't be possible if we don't believe in ourselves and in what we are doing.

Chapter 8: Think BIG

I don't know about you, but I see myself a millionaire in the next 5 year or so (maybe even sooner). I have big plans for myself, for my family, for living live to its highest levels of joy. How about you?

I am 23 years old right now (in 2015) and I must admit that nobody contributed to what I have today, but myself. Do you want to succeed and to achieve everything you desire? Then you need to make some changes in your daily schedule and in the way you think, and you need to build effective habits. All of this will help you move forward to what you wish for.

But...the first thing you will need to do before you start everything is to think BIG, to think positive. You need to go to the future inside your head and to see yourself successful. Then come back to the present and push hard towards that.

This is called dreaming, or seeing the big picture of yourself.

The more successful you think you will be (imagine that), the more you will achieve. Even if you achieve 70% of what you want, dreaming of more and more will increase your real achievements. This technique is used by a lot of entrepreneurs. I was born in February, so I am an Aquarius, the sign which is the biggest dreamer of all the others. I always see myself in the future, I always want to achieve more, and I always find new ways to motivate myself. (I will discuss more about motivation in a dedicated chapter.)

Even if you dream a lot, the key to your success is to take action. Every person wishes for something, but how many of us really take action and do something for their dreams? Most of us are pleased with a mediocre job, a mediocre house, a mediocre car (or none) and they do nothing for themselves.

Imagine yourself successful; think of how you can get there, build your own business and move towards that checkpoint before others do.

There are people in this world who have done this since they were kids. They work, they study, they are smart and they fulfill their dreams.

My motto in life is, "If he CAN do it, why CAN'T I?"

What does a successful person have compared to me? He has a brain, two hands and two legs. How did he manage to achieve success? Hard work, luck and commitment, and most of the times luck is made 90% by ourselves.

I like being different than others and I like to be discreet with everything I do. Work for yourself, in silence, achieve your goals and don't show everyone how "rough" you are.

Think BIG, start small, take action, commit yourself to something and don't give up. These are the "habits" which will lead you to fulfilling your dreams.

Chapter 9: Diversify your income

As an entrepreneur you will always have to be careful with your income streams. Don't invest all your time, money and energy into one single niche. This can be very dangerous just in case something goes wrong with the business that you run.

A wise man once said, "Don't put all your eggs in one basket" - from here we can see that this can be applied in any business that we do - don't invest all your money in gold, don't invest all your money in stocks, don't invest all your money in advertising, and make sure you split everything correctly and wisely.

The best way to diversify your income is to find similar niches which will save you in case something goes wrong, and find some niches that can help you grow your main business.

Let's take an example - let's say that my main business is Kindle publishing. If I do exactly as I mentioned earlier, I will make sure to invest in other additional income streams (I will create them) which will help me grow my main business (Kindle Publishing). So, I will use the following:

CreateSpace

YouTube

Audible ACX

Udemy

Amazon Kindle Direct Publishing

Amazon Associates

Amazon FBA

Google AdSense

Blogging

Facebook

Twitter

As KDP is my main business, I will use the other sources to diversify my income and also to grow my entire business.

With CreateSpace I will make physical versions of my bestselling books on Amazon, which can then be sold through the CreateSpace eStores, libraries and other physical places. Using this I will get more money, I will allow customers a new way to buy my book (in case they prefer the print version instead of the digital version), and I will also increase my popularity as an Author. If people liked the printed books which they bought from a physical store, they will surely find me on Amazon or on my blog, Facebook, etc. In other words, I increase my popularity, visibility and income. Generally, through CreateSpace you can earn 20-30% of your sales on KDP.

With YouTube, I can promote my books, increase my visibility, promote my blog, I can link my Facebook page and much more. By using it consistently, I will be able to get thousands of subscribers, thousands of views and thus, a couple of extra hundred dollars each month. In other words, I will earn more money (a new income stream) and I will increase my visibility and popularity. The money that I will be earning from YouTube will be from Google AdSense.

Audible ACX is another platform which is owned by Amazon and it helps me create audio versions of my books. A lot of people like audio books, as they can listen to them on their way to work, when they're relaxing, etc. It's a new and practical way to consume digital information. With this, again, I can increase my visibility and income.

Let's say that I learned a lot of things in 1-2 years of consistently publishing, blogging, learning, filming and earning money online. I would like to record myself while I am teaching something and thus, I will create an eCourse which will help a lot of people learn what I do. At the same time, I will benefit from this and I will sell them for a decent price like $99 or $199, or even $299 depending on the course. In this way, a lot of new people will find me on Udemy (or other platforms) and I will get more exposure, more sales of my books, more money from the courses and more money from the people who will visit my blog.

As an entrepreneur you will definitely need a blog on which you will engage all your loyal readers and followers who like what you do, what you teach and how you live. On your blog you can promote everything that you have - your courses, your books, your videos on YouTube, your Facebook page, your Podcasts, everything. With the help of a blog you will be able to generate money from Google AdSense, Amazon Associates and sales of your own products and books.

Amazon Associates will help you place some ads on your YouTube channel (descriptions, videos, etc.), on your blog, in your books, on your Facebook page; everywhere you would like.

If you want to go even further, you can sign up with Amazon FBA and create a physical product, advertise it and sell it on Amazon. The retailer will do everything for you - wrap, handle and ship it to the final customer. All you need to do is to find a supplier, a product, and some money to begin the process. Once the inventory gets to Amazon, you can start making money. There are people who are making a fortune just with this niche. The beauty of this is that you can manage everything from home and you don't have to deal with customers. It's a nice way to supplement your income.

Facebook and Twitter will help you grow your business, get visibility and increase your profits and your popularity. You can also pay for advertising and I highly recommend that you do so.

Now let's sum up - the income streams will be: Amazon Associates, Amazon KDP, Amazon FBA, Google AdSense (Blog + YouTube), CreateSpace, Audible ACX and Udemy.

When you will be able to generate enough money to buy a house or real estate properties to re-sell or rent, you can create another income stream which is 99% sure (the 1% is just in case a violent earthquake smashes your property or it catches fire). From real estate properties, you can get a monthly rent without any risks or major improvements to it. Even if the rent isn't too high for the price you pay for the house, I think it's a good investment as it will generate income no matter what happens to all your other online businesses.

Let's suppose that Amazon gets suspended or hacked and they can't work at all for 2 months. What are you going to do? Well, you will make decent money out of the blog, YouTube videos, courses on Udemy and probably from re-selling CreateSpace units through the platforms. You can also make money from the real estate properties that you own.

All these income streams except Amazon FBA will help my business grow the main business, which is Amazon KDP - I can get more readers from my blog, from my YouTube channel, from Udemy, from my Podcast, from Facebook, from Twitter, from CreateSpace and from Audible ACX.

To sum everything up - focus on one main business in which you invest more than 60% of your time and energy into, but also make sure you split the other 40% into other income streams. Focus on one thing, but don't put all your eggs in one basket.

Chapter 10: Spend less than you earn

Money, money, money. The tool for which we work and the tool which makes our lives better. How much money do we actually need in our daily lives? How much money should we spend to live decently?

The answer is simple - As much as possible!

Everybody wants more money, but the key to wealth is to spend less than you earn, no matter how much you earn.

An average person needs $1000 for bills and food, $1000 for rent/mortgage, another $500 for well-being, $500 for vacations and $500 for other personal stuff (clothes, gas for the car, electronics, parties, etc.). So this totals $3000 for a decent living. How much should you earn to cover all these safely?

You should earn at least $4000 to spend $3000 on what I mentioned. Of course, these expenditures can be reduced to $2000, especially if you own a house, you don't own a car and so on, but generally it's safe to spend 70-80% (maximum) of how much you earn.

As an entrepreneur, saving money is one of the keys to success, as it gives you the opportunity to invest more money and to remain financially relaxed during upir investments. It isn't wise to invest all your money in one thing, but it's advisable to invest as much as you can, without spending your emergency savings.

Pay yourself first

This principle is one of the greatest and it has been applied by most of the successful entrepreneurs and millionaires.

How does it work and what does it mean?

When you get your paycheck, dividends or whatever source of income that you earn, take a small percentage from the sum and FORGET about it. The percentage doesn't necessarily have to be big, at the beginning; 10% should be just fine. If you earn $3000, take $300 and put it into a savings account and forget about it - never touch it unless it is something really urgent or you have an opportunity to invest in.

Famous people like Warren Buffet used this principle but took it to higher levels - they were paying themselves first with over 50% and they invested that money.

Try to apply this principle to yourself no matter how much money you earn - if you manage to save $200 per month each month in 5 years you would save $12,000. This is just a small example.

If you're willing to become an entrepreneur, a millionaire, a mentor, you need to grow, to save money and to invest in your business and in yourself, so you need to come up with more than $200 each month.

Imagine that your business produces $10,000 per month net earnings. You take $4000 for yourself, you invest $3000 each month, and you save $3000 each month. That's a conversion rate of 30%, which is great. If you want to grow and become Warren Buffet, try following this rule.

If it's hard for you to keep up with these numbers, make automated savings to your bank account. Whenever a paycheck/payment is processed (to you) 30% of what you earn will automatically be transferred to a savings account. What's more interesting, you can sign up with your bank and you won't be able to take your cash for 12 months, 24 months, etc.

If we apply the example from above, in 2 years you can save $3000 x 24 = $72,000. This translates into more investments, a new luxury car, a real estate property, an online real estate, a nice emergency fund or money to travel for the next 10 years in exotic locations at 5 star hotels.

Let the money work for you

When it comes to business, investing, trading, and improving, you need to keep moving fast, and the only way to do that is to invest and outsource what you can. When I am talking about outsourcing, I am referring to hiring somebody to work for you, especially if there are simple tasks.

As an example from my Kindle publishing business - I hire freelancers to proofread my work, I hire freelancers to edit and format my book, I pay a designer to create my cover, and I hire a virtual assistant to help me promote the book. In this way, I invest, I get things done faster and I get my stuff done better. Those freelancers are doing one task, not 10, so they have more experience than I have. This is also a time saver; I can focus more on managing, writing, and planning the next steps. I make payments and schedule everything.

Yes, I could have done all of those by myself, but my time is limited. I can make a good cover in Photoshop in half a day, I can read my content twice and arrange it, correct any errors and such, I can promote my book when needed, but this will take me at least 4-5 days of working 8 hours a day without writing the content. Plus writing the content, I can go up to a month of work... For what? For $50-$200? It isn't worth it. By the time I finish a project by myself, I can outsource most of the tasks and I can grow faster, enjoy more time for myself and much, much more.

At the beginning I did everything by myself because at that time I had no money to invest. As I have started to earn money, everything has changed.

This is just my example. In other online businesses you can also invest in advertising, SEO, Google AdWords and so on. The key to growth is investing wisely.

Chapter 11: The 80/20 Rule

This famous rule is a major player for business owners, business starters and literally for everybody. It can be applied to everything - to health, life, goals, efforts, income, business, etc.

The origins of this rule came from an Italian, Pareto, who observed that 80% of Italy's income was being generated by 20% of the population.

This rule focuses mainly on improvement - how to improve your life, business, growth, productivity, time management, money management, way of thinking, and the amount of money that you earn.

In a business, 80% of your results will (generally) come from only 20% of your efforts or 80% of your outcomes will come from 20% of your inputs. I can say that in my own business, 20% of my products generate 80% of the total revenue and this will lead to a few things:

You need to focus on that 20% which generates 80% of your income - work harder on the 20% part, enhance it, upgrade it, maximize it. Don't spend time uselessly on the other 80% part of the inputs, which brings only 20% of the outcomès.

Apply this rule for optimal productivity - focus on the 20% of your project or service that really matters, while the 80% can be outsourced easily by hiring freelancers.

Example - you want to create a blog - 20% of the blog will be the ideas, quality, design, and marketing, while 80% will be the content, the proofreading of the content, the coding of the website and the maintenance. You can hire a ghostwriter to write down your ideas, you can hire a proofreader to edit and eliminate any grammatical errors, and you can hire a coder to make your blog responsive and clean. Focus on the tasks which an entrepreneur does - project management, money management, product development and marketing. All the other stuff can be done by hiring other people.

Don't get me wrong - you're not taking advantage by other people if you pay them $3/hour to write or $20 to proofread your work; this is just business, and you are helping others earn money. This is what they do, this is what they offer, and you don't need to feel bad because you earn 10 times or 100 times more money than the person who works 10 times more than you. This is another principle that I like which is "Work smarter, not harder".

This rule can be applied to marketing also. 20% of your clients will come back again, while 80% will come only once or twice. Focus on those 20% clients, engage them, give them stuff for free, and entice them to come again to buy your products or services. I am not saying to exclude the others, but offer your loyal clients (the 20%) a priority or an exclusive membership, whether it's paid or free.

There's a part of this rule where it should be reversed - instead of 80/20. Example - if you are creating new products or services which require 80% work that you don't like and only 20% you do, try to create a reversal - work only on projects which you 80% enjoy and 20% you don't.

P.S. - You can't work all the time at what you like. Example - I guess nobody likes to make calculations and predictions on how much tax you need to pay to the state, and I guess nobody likes to deal with negative feedback or other problems, but you have to solve them. Whatever you do, you will come across something you don't like to do; it's inevitable.

This rule is powerful if you understand how to apply it properly. Make a small study on what you do, what you earn and how your life is and try to apply this simple, but highly effective rule. Most of the successful entrepreneurs use this rule for their business and it has proved to be efficient.

Just search on the web how many people are actually applying this method in their lives and businesses.

Chapter 12: Review your work

A lot of business people and entrepreneurs tend to work for days, disorganized and without keeping an eye on what they're actually doing. The most important thing for self-improvement and for growing a business is to see some results. As soon as you put a lot of effort into finishing a task or a project, make sure to do a couple of things - review your work and keep an eye on your progress. Here's a short list of what you should do:

1. Look for mistakes - There's no such thing as perfection in this world. No matter how hard you try not to screw something up, you will make a few mistakes, whether they're minor or major. Now, the more experienced you are in what you do, the fewer mistakes you will be making. However, try to note all your mistakes down, highlight them, and try not to make the same mistakes again - put all your mistakes into a spreadsheet and analyze them carefully. Mistakes and failures are blessings from which you need to learn all the time.

2. *Time your work* - How much did it take you to finish your last project? Use timers to track your performance and compare it to the time required for finishing older projects. Do you see any difference? Note that down as well and track your performance.

3. *Take a closer look* - Look at your project and see what's missing - try to add details, enhance its overall performance and try to come up with new ideas for your next project.

4. *Compare results* - Compare each individual project and see how the results are evolving - positively or negatively?

5. *Create graphs and charts* - Make some charts for all your projects to see your overall progress in your business. This will help you know if you are on the right track.

6. *Review your work* after each project, each week, each month and each year. Compare your progress month after month and year after year. If you are on the right path, you should see small improvements.

7. *Compare yourself* with other competitors - how are your rivals doing? Analyze their flaws and try to create better projects, products or services which don't have their flaws. Try to design the best possible product or service.

8. ***Set checkpoints*** for your next project - as soon as you finish reviewing your current project, set some checkpoints, some goals for your next project so you can get started right away when you want to.

9. Reviewing your work shouldn't take more than 30 minutes each day - save your time for other important tasks and save your energy for important projects; reviewing your work should be something done by the end of the day before you go to sleep.

10. Organize everything carefully.

Chapter 13: Delay your lifestyle

Are you successful with your new business? Are you making a lot more money than you initially expected? Do you want to keep growing? Then don't do what I am about to tell you.

Some people have dangerous ways of 'celebrating' their success - they spend all their money fast.

Here's what the problem is - you are used to spending like $2,000 per month, so you need $2,000+ to fulfill your monthly needs. But, what are you going to do if you make $5,000? Are you going to raise your overall expenses to $5,000? It's up to you, but it will lead you to collapse.

You see, there are people in this world who win the lottery, they win $5 Million, $10 Million or more and in a couple of years, they are broke, they are in debt, they commit suicide, they get into jail and more.

The reason?

A lack of discipline regarding money management.

You need to 'delay' your lifestyle until you generate consistent and constant amounts of money through your business. When you will be going from $2000 to $5000, don't increase your expenses to $4,000 or $5,000; try to maintain them for several months at the same level as before.

I know it's difficult to live exactly as before when you see money rolling in, but try to spend your money on what is necessary; don't go immediately to change your car, or your house, or spend all your money by going on expensive vacations. This will immediately lead you to collapse, especially if you don't have a constant amount of money.

As an entrepreneur your earnings will fluctuate. Every month is different, so you need to determine a minimum earning for the whole year (look at 12 months before and analyze how much money you made each month, find out which is the minimum amount and based on that start spending money, but not all of it).

The same thing applies if you go from $10,000 to $100,000 per month. Don't go to buy a Ferrari; you don't need it anyways. Each of us have our own dreams and passions, but in business these need to be delayed. You need to learn how to discipline yourself.

Before you buy something just ask yourself 2 things:

1. Do I really need this?
2. If I didn't have that, what would happen? (If the answer is 'nothing', then you don't need it.)

When you go from $2,000 to $10,000 and then you see a constant growth to $12,000, $15,000, $20,000 and so on, you can safely increase your expenses to $4,000-$5,000.

These are just some numbers which came into my mind now; what I wanted to underline is the idea that you must not fall into this trap. If you want to grow and to be financially free and safe, you need to delay your lifestyle. Buy what you need, spend less than you earn, save money for future investments (for growing your business) and keep working.

As I said with the lottery, those people get into debt really quick just because they don't invest, they don't save that money, and they don't keep their same standards. They go from $2,000 to $5 Million and they instantly go and buy luxurious cars and mansions; they 'enjoy life', but that joy is very limited.

To sum this up, money isn't for everybody - there are few people who are able to build a business or who are able to manage money properly and wisely. Most of the people spend everything they have and some they don't - they get into massive debt.

It's always advisable to spend the money you have; don't get loans unless you need a mortgage or you need money to support an outstanding business idea. Getting loans for buying new things, especially cars, is the worst thing you can do. You literally buy what you can't afford by yourself.

The time when you will succeed will come. Be smart and delay your lifestyle!

Chapter 14: Distractions and negative factors

I am sure that all of us at least once had an extraordinary idea of some kind which could have changed our own lives, but it was smashed by parents, friends, haters, or any person who just didn't agree with that idea.

If your goal is to become a successful entrepreneur, it means that you have to put a lot of effort into it and leave everyone behind. Surround yourself with successful people, positive thinkers and things which make you happy.

Ignore 'toxic' people

If you're planning to start a new business or you already started one I am 99% that you will come across people who don't agree with your ideas at all.

The worst part here is that most of these people are jealous; they hate you because you are different, just because you have a bright idea. These people can be anybody - your closest friends, your family, strangers, competitors; these are 'toxic' people who want to influence you negatively in making the right decisions.

You will probably hear things like, "Are you out of your mind? Go find a job and forget about your crap ideas," even from your parents. Even though your parents will support you in anything you will do, they are too old to understand the opportunity that you have.

You need to strike the iron while it's still hot. You need to prove to everybody that they're wrong and what you are doing is great. I am not saying to ignore a person who gives you advice, I am saying to ignore those pathetic people who just want to drag you down without any reason.

My parents were dreaming that I would one day become an engineer, just like them, and I did, but I have never worked as one and I will never do so. Why? Because I found out by myself that there are a lot of people who earn 100 times more money than I would earn as an automotive engineer and I simply switched to online entrepreneurship.

I love cars, I love math, I love science, I love to work, but in the country where I live I can easily do anything else than that and earn twice as much with two times less effort.

My parents thought I was crazy, my cousins said that I was stupid... Other people were influencing me negatively... All of this until I got my first $1000 payment from Amazon and then they were beginning to see the potential.

Even then they were telling me that this can disappear at any time and then what am I going to do? They may be right, but if you are committed enough and you put a lot of effort in what you do, there are only small chances of failing. The key here is to always invest and to spend money wisely.

No matter how good you are at doing something, some people will eventually hate you. No matter how stupid you are, some people will eventually like you. What I am underlining here is that you can't please everybody; there will always be somebody who will be against your will. You need to get over that when it does happen, as it will inevitably happen to all of us.

The internet is the number one tool in human history which has made people millionaires, and it will be like that more than a century from now. It's the key to our evolution, even if it has some negative parts.

When people try to influence you negatively, make sure to prove that they're wrong. You don't have to give up easily on yourself, on your dreams, or on an idea that can change your whole life.

It feels great to see how you are different than 90% of the people you see. It's amazing to go where you planned from the very beginning. It isn't easy, and it won't happen overnight, but it can be done.

What I realized is that the beginning is the most painful. It's difficult at first to get used to a new schedule, to come up with new ideas, to take risks, and to wait for the money to come in, but once you get used to it, you will love what you do.

People are always afraid of what they don't understand. People are always judging things or other people before you finish what you have to tell them. Not everyone is open-minded. I consider myself an open-minded person and if you want to achieve success, you also have to be open-minded.

Of course that there are haters and 'toxic' people who will always influence you negatively when they are seeing that you earn 10 times more money than they do, you work whenever you want, you do whatever you want, you don't have a boss, you don't go to work from 9 to 5, and that you are totally different. When you are different from all the others, they will see you as a weird guy, a thief or a scammer. Things don't work like that.

I see a lot of teenagers, young people and even adults who are playing video games all day long or in their free time. Just in case you didn't know, video games are meant to manipulate the masses; playing games won't bring you any benefits for your business.

I've seen people who are making gameplays of famous games and uploading them on YouTube, from which they get paid. There are also 3D artists who have to test the games before they go live, but these cases are rare. Most of the people who play games for hours every day will not have a bright future.

This is just a small example. What I am saying is that you have to avoid the ways that you can be manipulated - TV shows, social media (posting silly things all day), playing games all day long (with no purpose), alcohol, drugs, too much partying, and people will all distract you from your goals, from your work. If you do all these just occasionally, it's OK, but if you have an addiction to them, well, you need to find a way to cure yourself if you want to succeed in life.

An online entrepreneur has to understand all these concepts and has to get through them; you have to ignore every negative thought, person, and thing that will drag you down.

I am not saying that if you ignore the distractions you will succeed, but if you want to succeed, you need to focus on what you need to do. Never give up on your dreams, work hard and shift your life to something much, much better.

Now I am sure that you will now wonder - "Then what should I do to enjoy my life? No TV, no games, no silly stuff, no social media, no distractions, then how am I supposed to spend my time or how can I relax?"

I may have some answers - go jogging, go watch a movie, go on holiday, explore the world, travel, learn new things all the time, go on a date, go swimming, go out with your family, walk the dog, go shopping, play football, play tennis, go to a concert, etc.

Do things which have a positive influence on your life. Don't waste your time with useless things.

Chapter 15: Help other people

For every company or business, the purpose is to offer goods or a service for other people, whether the service is physical or digital. Poor services and poor quality products are immediately going down due to several factors, which can include bad reviews, word of mouth, competition in the market, lack of money and lack of experience.

As an entrepreneur, you will be able to scale up your business long term only if you deliver value to people. Generally, when a person is looking forward to buying something, they want exactly what is said in the description. What's even more interesting, products and services which offer even more than they promise (like a bonus or gift) convert better into profits and scalability.

The main thing which you need to understand here is that you need to feel your customer's needs and try to really solve their problem. You need to be honest and to really love what you are doing, what you are offering. If you're trying to be honest or you are trying to solve somebody's problem, but you don't manage all the time to do it, then you won't succeed. A real entrepreneur with a business has to please 99% of their customers in order to succeed, grow, become popular and make money.

Helping people will also bring you satisfaction and the motivation to keep working on your business; it will give you the power to grow faster and more efficiently. Just think of the opposite scenario, in which you sell some products to 100 people, of which 80% are not satisfied. They get pissed off, they leave negative reviews, they request refunds, they tell other people not to buy it, etc. This will only drag you down, instead of growing.

If your goal is to build up a serious brand, a company, you will need customer support and you have to train your employees on how to deal with any unpleasant situations.

In any business, it's very important to give things away for free, and even when you offer something for free you will need to deliver value to people. It's pretty simple - if somebody gets something for free from you and you helped that person, without any doubts that person will come back to you for more and they will be willing to pay more. I will discuss more about this subject in the next chapter and I will present a technique.

Chapter 16: Take failure as a blessing

There is no such thing as perfection. There is no such thing as 'failure', only bad results. Take these results as a new lesson from which you learn something new.

Every time you try something out, every time you take some risks, you will gain experience and knowledge and you will improve yourself. I can say that I've used dozens of methods in my businesses - some of them worked, some of them didn't. What I've learned from these is to keep the best ones and to try to improve the ones that didn't work well. So, don't exclude any ways which didn't bring you satisfaction, but try to find a way to make that method work.

Example - in my publishing business, I have used several ways to promote my books. Some ways were effective, some of them weren't. But I found out that if I make a few improvements and I combine the methods that work with the new and improved 'failed' methods, the results were almost doubled.

Failure is something which we need to embrace. This is what business is all about - how much 'failure' are you able to withstand until you become successful? Even if you have the right mindset, but you feel down and you think of quitting after your first 'failure', then you are not suitable for entrepreneurship. You can still try to improve yourself and to learn from every mistake that you make.

To take advantages from all of our mistakes when we run a business, we need to make a sheet, a table with all of our experiences, failures and successes each month and each year. We need to know how our evolution will be - did we grow? Did we go down? Why? What caused our success or our 'failure'?

Everything needs to be tracked and taken into consideration.

Every human makes mistakes; it's something left to us from Mother Nature. The only thing that we need to understand is that we have to avoid making the same mistake again.

Chapter 17: Reward Yourself

Work, work, work. That's what will keep pulling you up towards achieving success. Until you reach success, you may need to take a break, a short vacation or a day off.

When is it recommended to do this? Well... Set goals for a new project, work as hard as you can to achieve them and as soon as you finish, celebrate. Go on a vacation, or take a day off. Spend some free time in which you relax your mind and body for the next project, the next product, or the next step in your career.

I've seen people who just work hard and they don't take weekend off, vacations or any breaks just because they are cheapskates and selfish people. The worst part in this is that they're selfish with themselves.

To enhance your creativity, health, well-being and everything, you need to celebrate the work you've done, no matter what the results are. Life is short, so we need to fulfill our dreams, to work hard, but we also need to enjoy it. Just working endlessly for some goals, vanities, challenges or big numbers is all useless if you don't enjoy what you've built.

The best way to recharge your batteries, your health, and your mind is to be grateful and proud of what you've achieved until that moment and to live those moments with the "Work" and "Grow" buttons in idle for a short period of time.

Travel, run, go to the beach, swim, go shopping, go drive a car, play football, watch a sports match, go out with your family or your girlfriend and do anything that makes you happy and relieves stress at the same time. Believe it or not, rewarding yourself in one way or another helps you a lot in your business and it also makes you feel that you are a human being, and not a robot.

In spite of this rewarding sequence which needs to be a part of your life, remember that you have a business to run, a "job" to fulfill and a mission to accomplish, so don't waste too much time.

All these breaks and vacations need to be scheduled very carefully, and as I told you, the best times to do this is when you finish a project. Don't go to another continent when you're in the middle of working on a big, profitable project or product.

Most of the successful entrepreneurs do this. I also did this; as soon as I finished my 3rd book on Kindle, I took my girlfriend and we went to Rome for 5 days. It was a marvelous experience. We visited the whole place, we met new people, we took nice photos, we ate traditional Italian foods, and much, much more. It made me feel grateful for what I am doing, for what I have accomplished, and it gave me motivation and power to keep fighting for what I desire.

Rewarding yourself always needs to be an extra source of inspiration and motivation, so I highly advise you to take at least 3 days off every month, and every 3-6 months to go on a vacation (for a week or two).

Don't be just a robot; go and enjoy life too.

Chapter 18: The best way to promote a product or a service

Okay, so you created a business, you are on your way to becoming a successful entrepreneur, you created a few products or a few services and now you might think, "How can I promote all of these?"

Honestly, by far, the best way to promote a product is to create a new one.

Let's take it from the beginning and let's give some examples. You are a singer - you have 50 songs which are nice but nobody discovered you. You release more and more and new people find you - the new subscribers will check out your other songs and you automatically promote all your songs by releasing other new ones.

The same principle applies for websites, services, physical products, courses, books, etc. By the time that I have 50 business books in a few years from now, every book that I have released will make people click on my account and go to other books of mine which they may be interested in.

It's just a matter of time; the whole idea here is to keep working on your new projects, products or services. Never settle down.

Quality has an important role in this process; if you don't create good quality products, you will eventually fail. If you design a product which helps people and it's excellent, that product will speak for itself and its reputation will spread quickly, so quality will always stand out in front of others.

Advertising – combining quality with advertising equals success. Always invest in advertising whatever you create. I've seen products which aren't that good, but the company invested in advertising so much, that a lot of people buy it just for the trend.

Let me give you an example – Beats Audio Headphones. They are good headphones, they sound great, but they are way too expensive.

The reason behind this is that the company invested 70% of the money in advertising and only 30% in the product development process. On the opposite end, there is a company called Audio Technica, which sounds a lot better than Beats and it's cheaper. But... Have you ever heard of Audio Technica? My guess is no, as only a few people know about it. The quality of those headphones is the same as Beats for a price which is 3 times smaller or for the same price as Beats, you get a greater quality of the headphones.

As the company has other sound equipment such as microphones, DJ equipment and other products, they don't invest too much money in advertising and the result is visible – a company such as Beats is more popular.

Don't get me wrong, Beats is awesome, the headphones sound great, but not for the price they're charging.

Chapter 19: Summary & Applicability

In this chapter I will sum up everything that I presented above – step by step for those who do not own a business and want to start one.

1. **Come up with an idea** – for an online business, a physical business, or one that combines both; it's up to you. I would personally choose a full online business as it gives you the freedom to travel anywhere and the possibility to scale it up the way you want.

2. **Start right away** – Don't waste your time, just start. You don't need to make everything perfect; changes that need to be made can be made on the go.

3. ***Ignore anyone who stands in your way*** – Haters and negative influencers will always exist, but just ignore them and keep working.
4. ***Set goals for yourself and for your business*** – Make monthly and yearly goals and try to stick to them – this will help you grow fast and efficiently.
5. ***Make a schedule for yourself*** – Make sure to create a schedule which allows you to sleep and eat properly, to work and to have time for other personal activities.
6. ***Wake up early*** – All the successful entrepreneurs have this habit and you should adopt it too, if you haven't already.
7. ***Think about your success*** – You need to go into the future to see yourself as successful. Then, come back to the present and do

whatever it takes to get there. Imagine yourself being successful.

8. ***Save money*** - Invest & grow. Investing money will help you expand faster and make more money.

9. ***Help other people*** – Deliver value to people and they will love what you do. It doesn't matter what you're doing, just remember this step.

Other Books by Ryan Stevens

Amazon Associates Affiliate Program (click here on the photo for quick access)

Amazon Associates Affiliate Program May 16 2015
by Ryan Stevens

Paperback
$8.99 √Prime
Get it by Tuesday, Aug 11
More Buying Choices
$6.30 used & new (10 offers)

★ ★ ★ ★ ★ ▾ 29
FREE Shipping on orders over $35
Books: See all 75,274 items

Kindle Edition
$3.71
Auto-delivered wirelessly

This book is a quick guide for beginners and it presents the advantages and disadvantages of Amazon Associates – it's a step by step guide with all the resources that you need to start a business using Amazon's Affiliate Program. If you already own a website, you have it set up and you generate money using an affiliate program, then you won't find this book helpful.

Kindle Publishing PRO – Complete Expert guide

(click on the picture for quick access)

This book takes you from A to Z – from setting up to the point where you make money. This guide is for anybody who wants to start publishing or for anybody who is already into this business.

Resources, illustrations, examples, and experiences of my own are shown throughout the book.

Write a review

I am not sure if you know, but reviews are very important for my book, for my growth, and for improving myself and my books.

I kindly ask you to write a short review – rate it 1 star if you didn't like it at all, or 5 stars if you really enjoyed it; every opinion matters.

Let me know what you think about it and also let me know what you would like to know more about.

Note – Before leaving a negative review be aware that I will constantly improve the books and add new information every 3 to 6 months; you will be notified by email by Amazon about any updates.

Conclusion

I hope you enjoyed the book. I hope that you learned a few things from it and I hope that one day you will become a successful entrepreneur.

If you bought this book because you want to make a change in your life, I congratulate you for taking action.

Don't wait too long to start your own business. If you don't do it, others will, so take action now!

www.ingramcontent.com/pod-product-compliance
Lightning Source LLC
Chambersburg PA
CBHW070905180526
45168CB00005B/1930